Everything
You Need to
Know About

Deafness

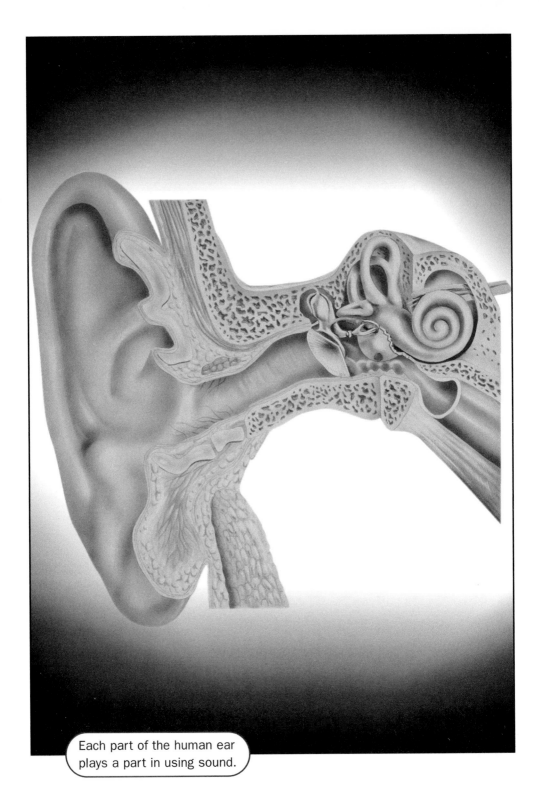

Each part of the human ear
plays a part in using sound.

Everything You Need to Know About

Deafness

Carol Basinger

Rosen Publishing Group, Inc.
New York

Published in 2000 by The Rosen Publishing Group, Inc.
29 East 21st Street, New York, NY 10010

First Edition

Cataloging-in-Publication Data

Basinger, Carol
    Everything you need to know about deafness/ Carol Basinger.
      p.   cm. — (The need to know library)
    Includes bibliographical references and index.
    Summary: This book discusses the causes of deafness, the types of deafness that can be identified, the effects of deafness on people's lives, and the help that exists for the hearing impaired.
    ISBN 0-8239-3165-X
    1. Deafness— Juvenile literature.   2. Deaf— Juvenile literature.   [1. Deaf 2. Physically handicapped]
617.8—dc21

Manufactured in the United States of America

17.96

Contents

	Introduction	6
Chapter One	**Human Ears and Normal Hearing**	9
Chapter Two	**Types of Deafness**	19
Chapter Three	**Causes and Prevention**	24
Chapter Four	**Communication**	34
Chapter Five	**An End to Isolation**	47
	Glossary	58
	Where to Go for Help	60
	For Further Reading	62
	Index	63

Introduction

*I*t wasn't a front-page story, but Maria still found it very interesting. The newspaper article said that deaf students at Gallaudet University in Washington, DC, were celebrating the tenth anniversary of King Jordan as the president of the university. Many of the students said that Jordan was the most important president in the history of the school.

Jordan had been an excellent president of the university, but his importance came as much from who he was as from what he had done. Founded in 1864, Gallaudet was the first liberal arts college for deaf people. In 1989, student protests at Gallaudet shut down the university. What did the students want? After 125 years, they felt it was time that the university was run *by a deaf president. After days of protests, the university agreed, and Jordan, who had been deafened at age twenty-one, was named the first deaf president in the history of the school.*

Maria was fascinated by the reasons the students gave for wanting a deaf president. Although she was a little embarrassed to admit it, Maria had not even realized that deaf people went to college, let alone that there was a university devoted to their education. She had never known a deaf person, but she had always assumed that deaf people were handicapped— that they probably could not do all of the things that "normal" people could. She assumed that they could not attain the same level of education as hearing people. Many of them could not even speak, right? Wasn't that the origin of the phrase "deaf and dumb"?

From the article, Maria learned that not only did deaf people not necessarily consider themselves handicapped, but that many deaf people considered themselves to be members of a distinct culture. Rather than consider their deafness a disability, they regarded it as a badge of distinction that allowed them to be in the world and perceive it in different ways than other people. So strong was this belief in some deaf people—or Deaf people, as those in the culture preferred to be known—that they even rejected technological and medical advances that would allow them to hear. One Deaf person put it this way: "Asking me if I want to hear is like asking a black person if she wants to be white."

Maria did not really understand this last point—if you could not hear, wouldn't you want to if the opportunity presented itself?—but it made her think nonetheless. Maybe, she thought, she had a lot more to learn about the so-called disabled and about deaf people in particular. She decided to start learning right away.

Chapter One

Human Ears and Normal Hearing

Ears work with sound. To understand human ears and normal hearing, we must understand sound. Also, to understand hearing, we must understand the parts of the human ear and their functions. When we understand these two areas, we can then understand how healthy human ears allow us to hear and why the ears of deaf people do not.

What Is Sound?

All sounds are made by vibrations. A vibration is the back and forth movement of an object that has been struck or acted upon by an outside agent. The vibrating object does not have to be solid. For example, wind, which is just air moving, makes a sound.

9

Lightning causes air to move, producing thunder.

The number of vibrations per second is called the frequency of the sound wave. The frequency is measured in hertz (Hz). One hertz is one vibration per second. Most humans can hear sounds with frequencies from about 20 to 20,000 Hz (20 to 20,000 vibrations per second). A human voice can produce frequencies from 85 to 1,100 Hz; jingling keys range from 700 to 15,000 Hz; a piano ranges from 30 to 15,000 Hz.

High and low sounds are identified by the word "pitch." In a drum set, the bass drum is a low pitch and the cymbal is a high pitch. How rapidly an object vibrates determines the pitch of the sound it emits. High-pitched sounds are created by objects that are vibrating rapidly; a lower pitch means a less rapid vibration.

Other words used in describing sound are "amplitude" and "intensity." Amplitude refers to how wide the vibrations are within the object making the sound. Intensity refers to the amount of energy flowing in the sound. The widest (largest) amplitude makes the most intense (energetic) sound.

A common word in talking about sound is "loudness." The human ear reacts differently to different amplitudes and intensities. If a high-pitched sound, middle-pitched sound, and low-pitched sound all have the same amplitude, the middle-pitched sound will seem the loudest to a human. The loudness of a sound changes with the distance the sound travels. A person close to the source of the sound (the vibrating object) hears the sound as louder than does a person farther away. This is because as a sound wave travels, it loses amplitude (strength).

A decibel (dB) is the unit used to measure the intensity (energy) of a sound. A decibel is not a measurement like inches and feet but a ratio. Zero decibels is the softest sound a human can hear. Increases in loudness are measured in relation to that zero. The increases are usually described in levels of ten, with each level meaning the sound is ten *times* louder than the sound a level lower.

The Parts of the Human Ear

Each part of the human ear plays a part in using sound. The parts are the outer ear, middle ear, and inner

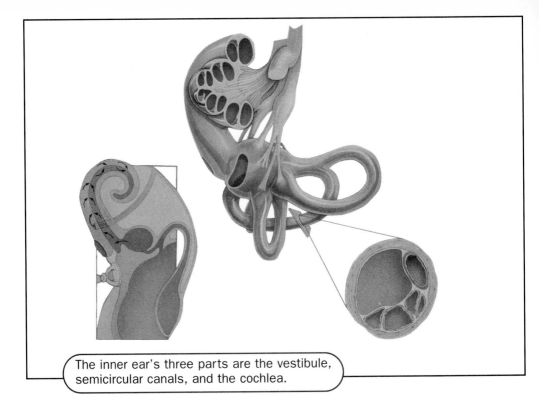

The inner ear's three parts are the vestibule, semicircular canals, and the cochlea.

ear. The outer, or external, ear includes the pinna, or auricle, and the external auditory canal. The pinna is the flexible, curvy thing we see on the outside of the head. It is made of skin and cartilage (a tough tissue that is not as hard as bone). The parts that make up the pinna have names. For instance, the outer rim of the pinna is the helix, the smaller rim inside of the helix is the antihelix, and the flat spot before and above the opening in the ear is the concha. Most of us do not recognize these names at all. Probably the only name we recognize is that of the fatty part to which some of us attach earrings: the earlobe.

The external auditory canal is the opening from the pinna into the head. It is approximately one inch (2.54 cm) long and lined with skin. The first one-third of the canal is made of cartilage. The skin of the pinna contains hair and glands. The glands produce sweat and wax. The inner two-thirds of the canal is formed by the hardest bone in the body, the temporal bone, which also forms the sides of the skull. At the end of the canal is the tympanic membrane, or eardrum. The eardrum is approximately two-fifths of an inch in diameter.

The middle ear is approximately .52 inches (1.3 cm) across and is made up of three bones and an opening to the throat. The bones connect the eardrum to the inner ear. One end of the malleus, or hammer, bone is attached to the eardrum; the other end of the malleus is attached to the incus, or anvil, bone. The incus, in turn, is connected to the stapes, or stirrup, bone. The base, or footplate, of the stapes is approximately .13 square inches and is connected to the oval window, a membrane that leads to the inner ear. Below the oval window is the round window. Both the oval window and the round window are actually in the wall of the cochlea, in the inner ear. The opening to the throat and nose is called the eustachian tube.

The inner ear is made up of three parts: the vestibule, semicircular canals, and cochlea. The vestibule is a small, round chamber approximately one-fifth of an inch long. It contains two membranes next to the middle ear: the oval window, to which the footplate of the stapes is connected, and the round window, which is just below the oval window. These membranes are a part of how the ear works with sound.

Blowing your nose opens the
ear's eustachian tube.

Also within and behind the vestibule is the ear's organ of balance, which does not play a role in the way the ear processes sound. Within the vestibule are two sacs, somewhat similar to balloons, called the utricle and saccule. The insides of the sacs are lined with hair cells that are attached to nerve fibers.

Behind the vestibule are the semicircular canals, each canal forming two-thirds of a circle and each canal connected to the others. Within each canal is a fluid-filled duct (tube) with an ampulla (pouch) at one end. Within the pouch are hair cells that are attached to nerve fibers. The tubes of the semicircular canals are attached to the utricle, which in turn is connected to the saccule. Movement of the fluids affects a person's sense of balance.

The cochlea contains the actual organ of hearing. The cochlea is shaped like a snail shell, coiling around its tip two and a half times, and is approximately the size of a pea. Within the cochlea are three fluid-filled ducts. One duct starts at the round window; the other duct starts at the oval window. They join at the tip of the spiral. Lying between the two ducts is the third duct, called the cochlea duct. Within this third duct is a membrane, called the basilar membrane, that has over 15,000 hair cells. It is these hair cells that make up the organ of hearing, called the organ of Corti. Lying above these cells is another membrane, called the tectorial membrane.

The auditory nerve completes the ear. It is split, with one branch, the cochlear nerve, starting from each hair cell in the organ of Corti, and the other, the vestibular nerve, starting from the hair cells in the pouches of each semicircular canal and the hair cells of the utricle and saccule. The two parts join to become the auditory nerve, which travels to the brain. There it divides in half, with one half going to each side of the brain. This nerve, with 30,000 neurons, is also called the acoustic nerve, or the eighth cranial nerve.

How Does a Human Ear Use Sound?

The outer ear works in hearing by assisting in determining the location of the sound source. The outer ear

15

collects sound waves and directs them through the external auditory canal to the eardrum. The external auditory canal becomes smaller as it gets closer to the eardrum. This decrease causes compression of the sound waves and makes them stronger. (They need to be made stronger because it is harder to move through the fluid of the inner ear than through the air of the outer and middle ear.)

Yawning, swallowing, or blowing one's nose opens the eustachian tube. The tube allows air to enter the middle ear so that there is air in both the outer ear and the middle ear. The sound waves hit the eardrum, causing it to vibrate. The eardrum vibrations cause the three bones of the middle ear to vibrate. The eardrum is so much larger than the base of the stapes that sound waves are strengthened approximately seventeen times.

When the base of the stapes vibrates within the oval window, it causes the fluid in the cochlea to form waves. As the stapes vibrates and the cochlea fluid moves in waves, the round window moves in and out. The cochlea fluid pushes against the basilar membrane and causes it to move. The hair cells on the basilar membrane move against the upper membrane (the tectorial) and, with the movement, the hair cells bend, thereby creating electrical impulses in the auditory nerve. Different hair cells respond to different frequencies of sound, depending on where in the

Pure tone tests can determine one's degree of hearing loss.

spiral tube they are located. The auditory nerve transmits electrical impulses of different frequencies and intensities to the brain, which decodes the sound. Sound waves can also reach the inner ear without going through the outer and inner ear, passing through as vibrations of the skull.

Put simply, vibrations create sound waves. The sound waves reach the inner ear and activate impulses in the auditory nerve, which then are decoded by the brain. We then say to ourselves, "Oh, I hear a baby crying," or "Here comes an ambulance; better move to the side of the road and let it through."

Chapter Two

Types of Deafness

The human ear's use of sound is very complex. It is not surprising, then, that identifying and treating the various types of hearing loss is also very complex. "Hearing impaired" is the proper general term to use when talking about hearing loss. "Deaf" and "hard of hearing" are categories of loss that fall under that term.

Identifying Hearing Loss

A person's level of hearing impairment is identified through the use of audiograms. The audiograms use pure tones (different frequencies and intensities) and speech (words and groups of words). People with special training, called audiologists, conduct the tests using soundproofed testing booths and special equipment called audiometers.

Speech and pure tone tests require responses from the person being tested, who lets the audiologist know what has been heard or understood. A response is given by pressing a signal, repeating words, or some other method. The tests do not work with newborns, infants, and unconscious patients. For those patients, two other forms of hearing tests can be used. One test, called the auditory brainstem response (ABR), follows nerve signals from the inner ear as they travel along the auditory nerve to the brain. The other test, known as otoacoustic emissions (OAE), relies on a peculiarity of the ear: As sound travels to the inner ear, low sounds are produced by the inner ear and can be heard by a microphone that is placed in the ear canal. Checking for those sounds can give clues to how the ear is working.

Types of Deafness

Audiograms also identify the types of deafness: conductive, sensorineural, and mixed. Conductive deafness is the result of something not working right in the outer or middle ear. Most cases of conductive deafness are due to problems with the bones of the middle ear. Sensorineural deafness is caused by a disorder in the inner ear or the auditory nerve. Mixed deafness is a combination of conductive and sensorineural deafness.

Tests for sensorineural deafness are done by placing earphones on the person's head and sending the pure tones through the air in the outer and middle ear to the inner ear. If a loss is found, the type of loss still cannot be clearly identified until a bone conduction test is done. The bone conduction test is done by placing bone vibrators on the person's head. Vibrations are sent through the skull directly to the nerves of the inner ear, skipping the outer and middle ear. If the person hears better with the bone vibrators, the audiologist knows that there is a problem with the outer or middle ear, and the person is said to have conductive deafness. If the person does not hear any better with the bone vibrators, the audiologist knows that the inner ear is not working and that the person has sensorineural deafness. Mixed deafness, some conductive and some sensorineural, can be identified with these tests.

A type of deafness that is not readily identified by audiograms is non-organic hearing loss (NOHL). It may be psychological in origin or pretended. In a psychological instance, there may be a true hearing loss that has destroyed a person's confidence in his or her ability to hear. The person lives as though he or she has a greater hearing loss than the actual impairment and even responds to audiograms in a way that indicates a greater level of loss. Emotional or psychological trauma is another common cause. For example, non-organic hearing loss sometimes appears as a symptom in soldiers who suffer from combat fatigue or post-traumatic stress syndrome. This response is not conscious and not faked. Pretended loss, which is faked or acted, is something quite different. It is more common where proof of the loss can result in awards of money. Pretended deafness can be exposed by audiograms.

Degree of Hearing Impairment

The audiologist checks what frequencies a person can hear and how intense a frequency has to be for the person to hear it. A chart is used for recording the test results. It shows the frequency levels across the top of the chart and the decibel levels along the side. When the test has shown how loud a sound has to be before the person can hear it, the audiologist finds the frequency across the top and moves down to the decibel level and marks that place.

The frequencies of human speech are shown on audiogram charts as 500, 1000, and 2000 Hz, but the audiologist also checks higher and lower frequencies. In determining the degree of hearing impairment, a formula is used that gives the average of the decibel levels needed for a person to hear the speech frequencies called thresholds. A person who needs a decibel level of 90 to hear 2000 Hz, 60 dB to hear 1000 Hz, and 10 dB to hear 500 Hz would have a pure-tone average of 53 dB.

Classifications of hearing impairment use these guidelines: A 0–25 dB threshold is normal; 25–40 dB is mild hearing loss; 40–55 dB is moderate hearing loss;

55–70 dB is moderately severe hearing loss; 70–90 dB is severe hearing loss; and 90–110 dB is profound hearing loss. People with thresholds of 25 to 90 dB are identified as hard of hearing; people with thresholds at 90 dB and above are identified as deaf.

Another method of classifying hearing loss is by percentages. It is typically used for medical and legal cases regarding hearing. More than one formula may be used. Again the thresholds at 500, 1000, and 2000 Hz are used. Hearing that is better at 26 dB is not thought to be a loss. Hearing that is below 93 dB is thought to be a total loss. Therefore, a scope of only 67 dB is used in calculating a loss from 0 to 100 percent.

What Is Heard

Between sensorineural and conductive deafness, there is a difference in the kind of hearing that is lost. Sensorineural losses tend to be in the high frequencies. The consonant sounds of human speech are high frequency, for example, so people with high frequency loss do not hear consonant sounds well and therefore have difficulty understanding speech. Often, conductive losses do not affect the high frequencies enough to cause a problem in hearing consonants. Some children with conductive loss are not immediately diagnosed as being hearing impaired because they do not seem to have a problem in understanding speech.

Chapter Three | Causes and Prevention

A normal ear uses its three parts (outer, middle, and inner) to change sound waves into signals that are sent through the auditory nerve to the brain, where they are decoded. When one or more of the parts of the nerve do not work right, hearing loss occurs. Birth defects, genetics, disease, drugs, injury, and aging can all cause hearing loss.

Birth Defects

Some babies are born with impaired hearing. There are many causes of such birth, or congenital, defects. Among the most common are a mother's use of tobacco, alcohol, and other drugs, such as cocaine, while pregnant. Not only illegal drugs have harmful effects; some legally prescribed medications can also cause damage.

A mother's illness during pregnancy can also cause

birth defects. For example, if a pregnant woman has measles, her baby may be born hearing impaired. Another danger to an unborn child is a condition known as toxoplasmosis, which a woman can contract from exposure to a parasite. The parasite may exist in cat feces, raw or undercooked meat, raw goat's milk, raw eggs, and insects. Almost all babies infected with toxoplasmosis develop complications years later, including hearing loss.

A condition known as Rh disease may cause sensorineural hearing impairment. Rh factors are antigens that are present in the red blood cells of most people (85 percent of whites, 93 percent of African Americans, and virtually 100 percent of Asians and Native Americans). An antigen is a substance that can trigger an immune response in the body. For example, under normal circumstances certain viruses or bacteria present in the body trigger an immune response, which is how the body fights off infection. In Rh disease, the mother and her unborn child have incompatible Rh factors, which sometimes results in antibodies in the mother's blood launching an immune response against the child. In such cases, the child can be born severely jaundiced and anemic and with other complications, including hearing loss.

Genetics

Genetics, or heredity, is a major factor in hearing impairment. Genes are found on the chromosomes of

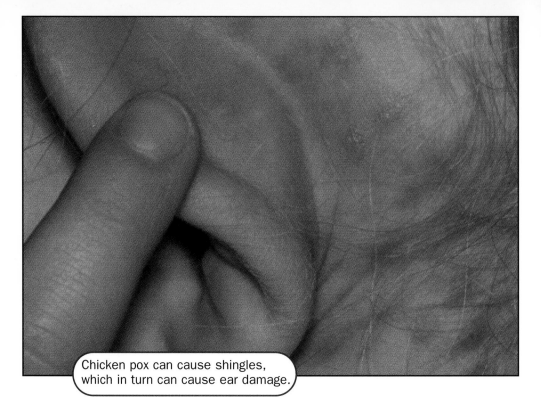

Chicken pox can cause shingles, which in turn can cause ear damage.

every cell in the body. The chromosomes contain genetic material known as DNA (deoxyribonucleic acid), which is what passes on the characteristics we inherit from our parents.

Experts have identified numerous kinds of deafness that are caused by inherited abnormalities. In about 60 percent of people with hearing impairment, the loss can be traced to defects in a single gene. About one child in every 1,000 is born deaf from genetic causes; another one per 1,000 will develop hearing loss from genetic causes later in life. Such impairment later in life may be caused by a genetic condition that makes a person more susceptible to various risk factors for hearing loss, such as noise, drug use, or infection. Genetics may also be a factor in various syndromes in which deafness is one of the symptoms, such as Pendred's syndrome or retinitis pigmentosa (deafness with goiter).

Disease

Otitis media—inflammation of the middle ear—is the second most common health problem in preschool children. (The common cold is first.) Usually with otitis media, there is a buildup of fluid in the middle ear. If the inflammation occurs repeatedly, damage to the eardrum, bones, and nerve of the ear can result.

Some diseases that are usually thought of as childhood illnesses also infect adults. Among them is chicken pox, which can indirectly cause hearing impairment. The virus that causes chicken pox sometimes reactivates and causes shingles. Shingles is a rash of blisters that may cause itching or pain. Ear damage can be a complication of shingles. Childhood diseases that may directly affect the ear are measles, rubella, mumps, and pertussis, which is commonly known as whooping cough.

Other illnesses that can cause hearing loss include Meniere's disease, meningitis, and autoimmune conditions such as lupus, rheumatoid arthritis, and diabetes. Benign or malignant growths in various parts of the ear may cause deafness. Otosclerosis is a growth affecting the stapes bone that prevents the stapes from vibrating. Without this vibration, sound is not sent to the inner ear.

The common hair dryer may be too loud for safe use.

Drugs

Some antibiotics are known to cause hearing loss, as can certain narcotics, especially when used in combination. One study has indicated that smokers have a 70 percent greater risk of hearing impairment than nonsmokers and that nonsmokers who live with a smoker are more likely to have hearing impairment than people who are not consistently exposed to tobacco smoke.

Injury

Injury is a common cause of hearing loss. A blow to the head can cause both conductive and sensorineural hearing loss, but exposure to noise is the most common cause of injury that leads to hearing loss.

Sound in the range of 20 to 80 dB is considered safe for hearing. The possibility of injury comes not just from the decibel level but also from the length of time the ear is exposed to the noise. The National Institute for Occupational Safety and Health has stated that the maximum time for safe exposure to 85 dB (for example, the sound of a motorcycle or snowmobile engine) is eight hours; for 110 dB (the sound of a jackhammer at a distance of two feet), that time is reduced to eighty-nine seconds. Noise above 85 dB will damage hearing through continued exposure; noise above 140 dB can damage hearing in only one exposure.

In the home, such common household devices as a vacuum cleaner, hair dryer, or garbage disposal may be too loud for safe use. At work, a handsaw, subway train, leaf blower, ambulance siren, or artillery fire (at 500 feet) may be too loud. Heavy traffic, a snowmobile, a busy video arcade, a symphony or rock concert, a balloon pop, or a handgun firing are other loud noises that can damage hearing.

In the United States, where farming is such a highly mechanized industry, seven out of ten farmers experience some hearing loss, with almost two-thirds having moderate to severe hearing loss. Some farm equipment is so loud that the longest a farmer may safely operate it without hearing protection is half an hour.

Some children's toys emit sounds as loud as 90 dB. The way a child plays with the toy can increase the

Decibel levels at football games and other large arenas may be damaging to your hearing.

effect. For instance, a child may squeeze a 90-dB toy while holding it close to his or her ear, thereby exposing the ear to 120 dB. Toys that may be dangerous include cap guns, talking dolls, walkie-talkies, musical instruments, and toys with cranks.

At rock concerts, the dB level right in front of the speakers may be 140 dB and less than 120 dB farther away. Other sources of potentially dangerous noise are boom boxes, bars and dance clubs, motorcycles, auto races, and monster trucks. In 1998, a professional football player said his ears rang for two days after a game. Depending on the shape of the arena, crowd noise in a stadium can be 120 dB.

Aging

In the United States, two-thirds of people over the age of 65 have some hearing loss. The loss may come from illness or excessive noise experienced earlier in life. Possibly there are changes in the auditory system or the brain caused simply by aging.

Prevention

Some kinds of hearing loss can be prevented. Any child that is suspected of having a hearing impairment should have auditory testing. Even when a child does not show signs of hearing impairment, auditory testing should be done during the first two years of school and routinely after that. Anyone in a family with a history of hearing loss should have annual hearing checks.

For hearing loss that comes from birth defects, the best means of prevention is for pregnant women to avoid the use of tobacco, alcohol, and drugs. Even if she does not smoke herself, a pregnant woman should avoid exposure to secondhand smoke. A pregnant woman should always consult a doctor before taking any kind of medicine, including over-the-counter medications.

Pregnant women should avoid potential sources of the toxoplasmosis parasite, such as cat litter boxes, garden dirt, raw meat, raw goat's milk, raw eggs, and insects that may have been around cat feces. Before she reaches childbearing years, a girl should be sure that she has been immunized against measles.

Scientists are learning new things about congenital conditions every day; a woman who is hoping to become pregnant should talk to her doctor about prevention. Parents can also receive genetic counseling that allows them to make choices about reproduction. A person with a genetic predisposition to hearing loss can take active steps to avoid sources of possible injury.

Parents and caregivers should get medical care for children who have ear infections. All children should receive immunizations against diseases such as chicken pox, measles, rubella, mumps, and whooping cough. For diseases for which there are no vaccines, such as Meniere's disease and meningitis, the best prevention strategy is knowledge of the symptoms and early medical treatment. Awareness can also serve to help lessen potential hearing loss in autoimmune diseases such as lupus, rheumatoid arthritis, diabetes, and others. Prevention can take the form of regular medical checkups and seeking medical attention whenever the ear does not feel right.

Wear protective helmets when in-line skating, bicycling, skating, skateboarding, or otherwise engaging in sports that could result in head injury. In a motor vehicle, use infant and child car seats and seat belts. Be aware that loud noise can be dangerous and wear ear protection whenever there is even a slight chance of hearing damage. Remove the part of a child's toy that makes noise. If that is not possible, consider getting rid of the toy.

Obviously, prevention does not work against aging itself. However, the standard preventive measures against hearing loss—regular checkups, avoidance of risk factors, and other good health procedures—should be taken.

Conclusion

Hearing loss has many different causes, including birth defects, genetic factors, disease, drug use, injury, and aging. Medical research into causes and treatments continue. The information provided in this chapter is only a small part of what is available. Some sources of information and help are provided at the back of this book, but it is important to remember that immediate medical advice should be sought for any suspected hearing impairment or susceptibility to impairment.

Chapter Four

Communication

There are several different ways to communicate with someone who is hearing impaired. They are speech combined with speech-reading (lipreading), writing, signing, finger spelling, or combinations of all of these.

What method or methods are used depends on the person's preference and the communication abilities of each person in the conversation. The preference usually depends on the schooling the person received and the person's age at the onset of the deafness. The degree of deafness also affects communication. The environment (noise, light, distance) and the voice qualities of different speakers can cause a person's preferred way of communication to change from moment to moment. Technology also affects how hearing-impaired people communicate.

Sign language is a true language with a unique structure.

Schooling

Before separate schools were established for the deaf, most deaf people lived in small communities, with their social contacts often limited to family members and other deaf people. Their communication took the form of whatever each person was able to develop for use within that group, including gestures. With the development of residential (live-in) schools for the deaf, a more uniform form of communication developed: sign language. As people graduated from the signing schools, they took their language to their home communities. The language then spread throughout their countries, and sign languages developed within each country. For the first time, deaf people from distant communities were able to communicate with each other.

Some schools for deaf people did not use sign language. Called oral schools, they focused on teaching deaf students a spoken and written language. The students were taught to recognize words by using what hearing they had and by speech reading. They were also taught to speak.

In the United States at the end of the nineteenth century, a great rivalry developed between educators of the deaf over the issue of whether deaf people should be taught to speak or to communicate exclusively with sign language. The two most prominent educators of the deaf were Alexander Graham Bell, who is perhaps

Alexander Graham Bell was a prominent educator of the deaf.

best known as the inventor of the telephone, and Edward Miner Gallaudet, the founder of Gallaudet College in Washington, DC.

Champions of oral education argued that speech reading and verbal instruction were necessary parts of learning to read and write successfully. Advocates of sign language, such as Gallaudet, pointed out that not all verbal sounds could be recognized through speech reading and that not all deaf people were capable of learning how to speak. Although neither Bell nor Gallaudet was in favor of the exclusive use of either sign language or verbal communication, the debate between them grew fierce. The two had developed a friendship based on their devotion to the education of the deaf, but their disagreement on the best methods of such education brought their friendship to an end.

By the 1960s, both methods had demonstrated mixed results. Three things were clear: Deaf people are as intelligent as hearing people; the visual clues for speech reading are not clear (50 to 60 percent of the sounds of English look like some other sound when spoken); and the average deaf student was leaving school poorly educated.

These facts led to the development and use of a method for educating the deaf known as total communication. As explained by Gerilee Gustafson, an educator of the deaf, total communication is "the use of a combination of manual signs, finger spelling, speech, amplification, speech reading, and any other means necessary to reach the child."

By the 1970s, studies had shown that American Sign Language, which is sometimes abbreviated as Ameslan or ASL, is a true language with a unique structure, vocabulary, and grammar. At about the same time, deaf people were beginning to look at themselves not as victims of a handicap or defect but as members of a unique culture.

Overt recognition of this culture sparked the use of the capital *D* in speaking of people who are deaf and who belong to that culture: Deaf. It continued with protest against the use of what is called manual English in the schools. Manual English is not ASL but a number of different systems in which total communication teachers create new signs for words in English. By contrast, deaf activists believe that creating new signs is their right alone because ASL is their rightful language.

Other methods of communication are also still used. Signed English, which is sometimes called Pidgin Sign English or PSE, uses the signs of ASL in the sequence of spoken or written English. In finger spelling, a person uses his or her fingers to create symbols for each of the letters of the alphabet and uses those symbols to spell out words. Some people use a method called cued speech to assist with speech reading. The cues help the speech reader to identify sounds that are easily confused.

Although the frequently used term deaf-mute implies that deaf people do not have the physical ability to speak, that is not the case. There are good reasons why a deaf person may choose not to speak. One common reason is that the speech of a deaf person may not sound like the speech of a hearing person. Some hearing people are startled by the sound of that speech and show their surprise. Sometimes a deaf person becomes tired of this reaction and therefore stops talking out loud. Another reason may be that speaking can be much harder than signing.

Age at Onset of Deafness

The age of a person when he or she suffers a significant hearing loss is the most important thing that determines how a deaf person prefers to communicate.

Two important terms are "prelingually deafened" and "postlingually deafened." The first term means that a person became deaf before learning a spoken language. The second term means that a person became deaf after learning a spoken language.

A prelingually deafened child who has not received any teaching or assistance in learning a written/spoken language may enter school knowing only a few words. By school age, the period of greatest natural language development is already almost over. A prelingually deafened child who begins school at this age must use his or her eyes rather than his or her ears to learn language. Because a child sees large movements better than small ones, sign language is easier than lipreading for a person to learn.

Many prelingually deafened people consider themselves part of the Deaf culture and prefer to communicate in ASL, which they regard as their native language. However, some prelingually deafened people learn spoken and written English and prefer to use it. In turn, some deaf people learn spoken and written English but then prefer to use ASL. Most every prelingually deafened person knows something of a written language. The level of writing skill varies greatly from one person to another. Some deaf people are comfortable using writing to communicate; some are not.

How postlingually deafened people choose to communicate depends on several factors. Perhaps the most important is the educational philosophy of the school they attend: oral school for the deaf, signing school for the deaf, residential school (students live at the school), day school (students live at home), or local school with various levels of attendance in hearing classes.

Degree of Deafness

The amount of hearing loss a child has is a factor in determining what school he or she can attend. Profoundly deafened children may be enrolled in schools for the deaf. Even some hard of hearing children may attend schools for the deaf. On the other hand, both profoundly deafened and hard of hearing students may attend local public schools along with hearing students. They may or may not attend special classes and may or may not receive special services.

People with sensorineural loss have often lost the high frequencies and do not hear consonants. If partial hearing of the frequencies remains, increased loudness may help with understanding. When the frequencies are completely lost, increased loudness does not help. Mixed hearing loss, of course, creates a mixture of the effects of conductive and sensorineural loss.

Environment

Noise, light, and distance from the speaker greatly affect the ability of deaf people to communicate. There is a form of impairment wherein some people actually hear better when there is background noise. This happens only with conductive deafness, where loudness helps some people understand speech. This better understanding may occur because people with normal hearing tend to speak loudly in noisy places. For most hearing-impaired people, however, noise is a severe handicap to understanding speech.

The noise of speech itself can prevent understanding. When people speak too rapidly, for example, the soft high-pitched consonants are overwhelmed by the louder low-pitched vowels. For people who are both deaf and blind, the amount of light available is not important to their ability to communicate. They may use special equipment for the blind, or sign language. The signing is done inside the person's cupped hands.

For other deaf people, however, lighting is critical. Lighting is necessary for seeing signs, for reading lips, for reading. The position of the light is important. A hearing-impaired person should not have to look into a light source, such as a window. When the speaker stands in front of a light, the speaker's face is not clear. A little forethought can prevent problems like this. In a restaurant, for example, a group can be sure that a hearing-impaired person sits with his or her back to a window. When making a slide presentation, the speaker can stand near the screen and let a light show on his or her face.

Many things affect how a deaf person may choose to

communicate. For example, in poor lighting, a person who normally uses speech reading may choose to switch to signing. In situations where no method seems to be working, the hearing-impaired person may ask the speaker to move someplace else—from a noisy room into a quiet hallway, for instance.

A common mistake people make when talking with someone who uses some hearing and speech reading is changing the words when asked to repeat what was not understood. The listener is trying to make sense of what was seen and heard. Changing the words makes the listener have to start over. It is best to repeat the whole sentence, word for word, once again. If the listener still does not understand, try changing an important word. The more syllables the speaker can use in a word, the better chance the listener has of understanding—for example, try changing "quarter" to "twenty-five cents."

Speak in groups of words. Hearing-impaired listeners are searching for the overall meaning of what is being said. They are trying to fit the misunderstood words into the context, or subject, of the sentence. For this reason, single words are extremely difficult to understand, as they are difficult to place in context.

To gain the attention of hearing-impaired people, turn the room lights off and on or stomp on the floor. If you touch a hearing-impaired person to get his or her attention, do so gently. Try to get into the person's line

Speech reading requires clear, face-to-face contact.

of vision before touching. Also, if you use touching to gain attention, try to limit how often you do it. Continual touching can become annoying.

Communication Assistance

There are a few medical procedures that can improve a person's hearing. Among them is surgery to free the stapes bone in the middle ear. Part or all of it may be replaced. A torn eardrum may be repaired, and a poorly formed pinna may be reshaped. The most complex of these procedures is a cochlear implant. A surgeon implants an electrode in the inner ear. A tiny microphone and sound processor pick up sound outside the ear and transmit it by a coil to the electrode, which is then able to stimulate the auditory nerve.

Hearing aids are a common technological device used by the hearing impaired. They are designed according to the type and degree of a person's hearing loss and work better in some situations and not at all in others, such as in places with a lot of background noise. Hearing aids work only when a person has some degree of hearing left.

Captioning enables deaf people with reading skills to know what is being said on television programs. Closed captioning is a feature that allows the TV viewer to see the a program's words spelled out across the top or bottom of the screen as a show progresses. In some cases, such as when the president of the United States addresses the nation, deaf viewers may be able to watch someone sign the president's words as he speaks.

Various technological advances now allow hearing-impaired people to use the telephone. Some people use handsets that allow the listener to adjust the volume. Hearing aids can be equipped with switches that allow the listener to use the phone. A TTY (teletypewriter) or TTD (telephone device for the deaf) allows a hearing-impaired user to communicate directly to another user. A TTY is like a small keyboard that uses computer codes to send messages through the telephone. Someone without a TTD may communicate with a TTD user through a relay service, which is now available in all states. Specially trained communication assistants relay the typed and spoken words between the callers. In recent years, an increasing number of hearing-impaired people have found the fax machine and e-mail to be useful and more private means of communication.

Special alarms are available for hearing-impaired people—for example, lights that flash when the phone rings or someone knocks on the door. In a car, a specially designed dashboard can visually indicate that a vehicle with a siren on needs to get through. Special alarm clocks can wake the deaf sleeper by vibrating the bed.

People can act as interpreters for the deaf. Family members and friends often serve as informal interpreters, but interpreting is also a profession. Certified sign language interpreters pass strict tests of their skills in changing English to ASL and ASL to English. There is certification in specialty areas such as law and medicine. Oral interpreters are specially trained and certified in making speech understandable for speech readers.

Hearing dogs can also provide assistance to the deaf. They are trained to alert hearing-impaired people when a baby is crying, a doorbell is ringing, and so on. Each dog is trained to meet the needs of the person he or she will serve. Hearing dogs wear identifying jackets when they are on duty. They have the same rights as Seeing Eye dogs, such as being allowed to go into restaurants, accompany their owners on public transportation, and so forth.

Chapter Five

An End to Isolation

Deafness affects communication. That may seem like a simple or obvious statement, but think of what it means for the deaf person. Every aspect of that person's socialization is affected: recreation; personal relationships, including family and romantic ones; education; employment; and overall ability to interact with the world. The result for deaf people can be a profound sense of isolation, with all the resulting consequences.

Social Interaction

Until recently, deafness was regarded as a defect, a shortcoming. Deaf people were viewed as not being as complete or whole as "normal" people. Many people assumed that deaf people simply were not as intelligent as those who could hear. From first diagnosis of

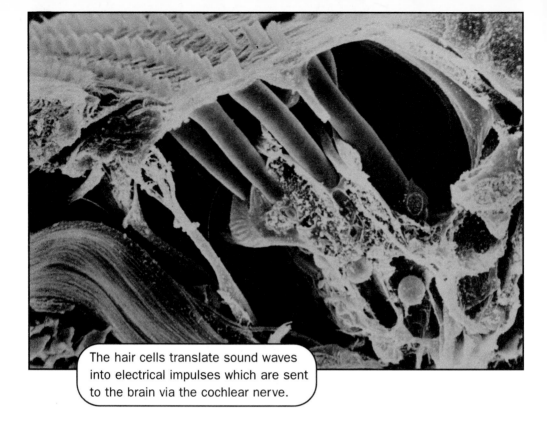

The hair cells translate sound waves into electrical impulses which are sent to the brain via the cochlear nerve.

impairment through death, a deaf person was viewed as being less than okay. Even the words most commonly used to speak of deafness—impairment, loss, problem, special, abnormal—all carried negative connotations. "Dummy" was a common nickname for deaf people that was generally considered to be acceptable.

It was attitudes such as these that the people of the Deaf culture have worked so hard to overcome. Instead of viewing themselves as disabled or handicapped, Deaf people emphasize their uniqueness. Some called themselves *differently abled* rather than disabled. Within the Deaf culture, being deaf is preferable to being able to hear. Deaf people often marry other deaf people.

People who grow up attending schools for deaf children often come to consider themselves members of the Deaf culture. Within that culture, they participate in many social, entertainment, athletic, and religious events. Bowling is a prime form of recreation within deaf communities. There also are athletic associations and world games. There are Deaf clubs wherein the members socialize, go on tours and cruises, square dance, and so on. There are theaters of the deaf where the actors and other members are deaf. There are many activities that both deaf and hard of hearing people enjoy. They include playing card and board games, playing in or watching sports, and dancing.

Aside from their effort to maintain control over ASL, an excellent example of the struggle of deaf people to define and establish themselves as members of a distinct culture is the debate over cochlear implants. For some infants and small children, a cochlear implant will allow them to hear, but deaf parents do not necessarily regard this as a good thing. As one Deaf woman explained in a newsletter, "I am a deaf mother and have a two-year-old hearing son. When he was born, I was hoping he would be deaf just like my husband and me. But when he wasn't, we accepted it and loved him just the same. When the son of our hearing friends Tom and Elly was born deaf, however, they had him undergo cochlear implant surgery so that he wouldn't be 'different' from his parents. Would it have been okay if I forced my son to have surgery that would make him deaf like us? No matter what, accept and love your child the way he or she is born."

People who suffer hearing loss or become deaf after their school years face a special set of problems in socializing. They have problems in the hearing world and the Deaf world. In the hearing world, their requests that speakers show their lips, speak more slowly, or repeat what was said are often met with impatience. In the Deaf world, they often struggle to learn a new language. Some Deaf people can be impatient and unaccepting of people who did not grow up in the culture. Being unfamiliar with both worlds, they often end up isolated.

Family Relationships

Deafness and hearing loss can place enormous stress on family relationships. The most obvious strain comes from the strain of communicating. In the case of a deaf child, for example, the hearing members have to learn ways to communicate with the child just as the child has to be taught ways of interacting with hearing family members and the rest of the world.

In the case of a gradual hearing loss, both the person who is losing hearing and the family need to adjust to the loss. Sometimes the loss is not even recognized at first. There may be feelings of resentment and anger.

There may be conflicts about what kind of education is best for the child. One person may blame another for the impairment. Sometimes the extra care a parent gives to a disabled child results in a spouse and/or other children feeling left out.

The hearing children of deaf parents may grow up understanding their parents' special needs and be willing to provide the necessary assistance. They may also, at times, feel pressured to give their parents special assistance even when they would prefer to devote time and energy to their own lives. The brothers and sisters of hearing-impaired people may also feel some of the same conflicts and pressure.

Education

As is true of any category of people, the level of education attained by deaf people varies greatly. Some deaf people drop out of school. Some gain graduate degrees. Reading is the most basic skill necessary for most levels of education and information gathering. Many prelingually deafened people have difficulty learning to read English. Thus many Deaf people rely on family members or interpreters for receiving their information.

The first school for the deaf was founded in Paris, France, in 1755. The first public school for the deaf in the United States, the American Asylum for the Deaf,

Academy Award-winning actress
Marlee Matlin is deaf.

was founded by Thomas Hopkins Gallaudet in
Hartford, Connecticut, in 1817. (Thomas Gallaudet
was the father of Edward Gallaudet, who founded
Gallaudet University in 1864.) Today institutions
devoted to the education of the deaf, with specially
trained teachers, can be found in virtually every major
city in the world. Gallaudet University in Washington,
DC, which remains this country's only institution of
higher learning devoted exclusively to the education
of deaf people. Not surprisingly, students at
Gallaudet have been in the forefront of the Deaf culture movement. In the late 1980s, they successfully
demonstrated to have a deaf educator appointed president of the college.

Spiritual Life

There are some religious organizations that are specifically of the Deaf. There are others that provide services for the deaf. Services of the deaf are organized and run by people of the Deaf culture. Services for the deaf are services for hearing people where interpreters are provided for deaf people. Both kinds of services are most likely to be found in large cities.

Employment

Because deafness can so profoundly affect education, communication, and social interaction, it is often difficult for deaf people to find meaningful employment. The most recent employment statistics are from Canada, where a 1998 survey showed that 37.5 percent of the 300,000 Canadians who use sign language are unemployed and 42 percent are underemployed (working below their knowledge and skill levels). The majority of the employed sign language users work in organizations that serve deaf people.

Depression

The most common consequence of the isolation that so many deaf people experience is the psychological condition known as depression. This may result in a reduced quality of life in terms of educational, economic, and

Heather Whitestone was the first deaf Miss America.

social achievement, as well as the ability to take part in and fully enjoy all the activities that lead to a fulfilling life. Studies indicate that depression and reduced quality of life are conditions twice as common among hearing impaired people as among hearing persons.

Depression can be as significant as deafness in reducing a person's ability to participate fully in life. Depression is not a mood or feeling that someone can simply "snap out of." Like anyone who suffers from depression, deaf people who are depressed need to seek medical and professional counseling. Many of the groups that provide services for the deaf can help in finding health care professionals who are specially trained in working with the deaf and their special problems. The names of some of these groups can be found at the back of the book.

An End to Isolation?

The hearing impaired. The hard of hearing. The deaf. The Deaf. All these names are missing one important word—*people*. The hearing impaired are people. The hard of hearing are people. The deaf are people. The Deaf are people.

These may sound like overly simple statements, but they are ones that society has taken centuries to fully accept. In ancient times, for example, people believed that the deaf lacked souls and the ability to think intelligently.

From the early seventeenth century well into the twentieth century, scientists and educators viewed deafness as a disease and believed that deaf people should be isolated from society, like the insane. Well into the twentieth century in the United States, deaf people were prevented by law from working for the U.S. civil service (that is, government posts) and were legally classified with criminals and insane people.

In the past several decades, deaf people have made enormous strides in gaining greater control over their lives. New technology, such as cochlear implants and hearing aids, have helped many deaf people to communicate more easily. The Deaf culture movement has increased pride among deaf people and raised the consciousness of nondeaf people. Classes in speech reading, finger spelling, lip reading, cued speech, and sign language provide deaf people with varied options for communication. Such classes can also turn into support groups and social opportunities.

A group known as SHHH (Self Help for Hard of Hearing Persons) helps the hearing impaired develop assertiveness and self-esteem. Marlee Matlin, a deaf actress, won the Academy Award for Best Actress in 1986 for her role in the film *Children of a Lesser God,* in which she portrayed a deaf student. More recently, Curtis Pride has excelled as a left-handed-hitting outfielder for several major league baseball teams, including the world champion Atlanta Braves.

The public success of such exceptional individuals raises public awareness of the special abilities of all deaf people, and there is no reason to believe that in years to come opportunities for deaf people will not continue to increase. As they do, the degree of isolation experienced by deaf people will lessen, and they can take an even more prominent place in society.

Glossary

amplitude Width of vibrations within an object making sound.

audiologist Scientist or technician trained in the study and treatment of hearing.

auditory brainstem response A type of hearing test usually performed on infants, newborns, or unconscious patients.

cochlear implant Surgical procedure in which a tiny electrode is implanted in the inner ear.

conductive deafness Deafness resulting from problems in the outer or middle ear.

decibel Unit of measurement of the intensity of a sound; its abbreviation is dB.

frequency For sound waves, the number of vibrations per second.

hertz Unit of measurement of frequency of sound waves; its abbreviation is Hz. One hertz is one vibration per second.

intensity The amount of energy within a sound.

mixed deafness Combination of conductive and sensorineural deafness.

otitis media Inflammation of the inner ear.

otoacoustic emissions A type of hearing test usually performed on infants, newborns, or unconscious patients.

postlingual deafness Loss of hearing after a person learns to speak.

prelingual deafness Loss of hearing before a person learns to speak.

Rh factors Antigens present in the red blood cells of most people.

sensorineural deafness Deafness caused by a disorder in the inner ear or the auditory nerve.

vibration Back and forth movement of an object struck by an outside agent.

Where to Go for Help

Gallaudet University
800 Florida Avenue NE
Washington, DC 20002-3695
Web site: http://www.gallaudet.edu
Gallaudet University operates the National Information Center on Deafness, a centralized source of up-to-date information on deafness and hearing loss. The center maintains state and national directories, which can also be accessed on-line.

Web Sites

Deafness Research Foundation
www.nfd.org

Deaf Resource Library
www.deaflibrary.org

Deaf World Web
www.deafworldweb.org

Hearing Speech and Deafness Center
www.hsdc.org

Magazines

Contact
Cochlear Implant Club International (CICI)
P.O. Box 464
Buffalo, NY 14223
(716) 838-4662

Deaf-Blind Perspective
345 North Monmouth Avenue
Monmouth, OR 97361
e-mail: klumphr@fstr.wosc.osshe.edu

Deaf Life
MSM Productions
Box 63083
Rochester, NY 14623
(716) 442-6370 TTY

Deafnation
P.O. Box 3521
Grand Rapids, MI 49503
(888) 332-3626 TTY
Web site: www.deafnation.com

Silent News
133 Gaither Drive, Suite E
Mt. Laurel, NJ 08054
(609) 802-1978 TTY
(609) 802-1977 Voice

For Further Reading

Lane, Harlan. *When the Mind Hears: A History of the Deaf.* New York: Random House, 1984.

MacKinnon, Christy. *Silent Observer.* Halifax, Nova Scotia: Kendall Green, 1993.

Sacks, Oliver. *Seeing Voices: A Journey Into the World of the Deaf.* New York: HarperCollins, 1990.

Schaller, Susan. *A Man Without Words.* New York: Summit, 1990.

Schein, Jerome D. *Speaking the Language of Sign: The Art and Science of Signing.* Garden City, NY: Doubleday, 1984.

Van Cleve, John V., ed. *Gallaudet Encyclopedia of Deaf People and Deafness.* New York: McGraw-Hill, 1987.

Walker, Lou Ann. *A Loss for Words: The Story of Deafness in a Hearing Family.* New York: HarperCollins, 1986.

Winefield, Richard. *Never the Twain Shall Meet: Bell, Gallaudet, and the Communications Debate.* Washington, DC: Gallaudet University Press, 1987.

Wright, David. *Deafness.* London: Faber & Faber, 1990.

Index

A

American Sign Language (ASL), 38, 40, 46, 49
audiologists, 19, 22
auditory brainstem response (ABR), 20

B

Bell, Alexander Graham, 36–37

C

causes of deafness, 24–33
    aging, 30–31
    birth defects, 24–25
    disease, 27, 32
    drugs, 24, 28, 31
    genetics, 25–27, 32
    injury, 28, 32
    noise, 27–30, 32
    Rh disease, 25
    shingles, 27
Children of a Lesser God, 56
closed captioning, 45
cochlear implant, 44, 49. 54
communication, 34–46, 47
    American Sign Language (ASL), 38, 40, 46
    finger spelling, 34, 56
    Pidgin Sign English, 39
    sign language, 36–37, 38, 40, 42, 45, 46, 53, 56
    speech-reading, 34, 36, 50, 56
conductive deafness, 20, 23

D

Deaf culture, 6, 38, 48–50, 55
deaf-mute, 39

deafness
    causes of, 24–33
    and children, 25, 26, 29, 31, 40, 49–51
    and communication, 34–46
    conductive, 20, 23
    and depression, 53–55
    and employment, 53
    identifying, 19
    non-organic hearing loss (NOHL), 21
    postlingual, 39–40, 51
    prelingual, 39–40, 51
    pretended or faked, 21
    prevention, 31–33
    and relationships, 47, 50–51
    sensorineural, 20–21, 23, 41
    and spiritual life, 52–53
    types, 19–21
decibels, 11, 22, 29–30
drugs, 24, 28, 31

E

ears
    parts of the human ear, 11–15, 24
    and sound, 15–17
education, 36–40, 51
    oral, 37, 40
    total communication, 38

G

Gallaudet University, 6–7, 37, 52
    student protests at, 6
Gallaudet, Edward Miner, 37, 52
Gallaudet, Thomas Hopkins, 52
genetics, 25–27, 32
Gustafson, Gerilee, 38

H
hearing aids, 45, 54
hearing dogs, 46
hearing tests
audiograms, 20–21
auditory brainstem response (ABR), 20
otoacoustic emissions (OAE), 20
pure tone, 17, 19–20
speech, 19
hertz, 10, 22

J
Jordan, King, 6

M
Manual English, 38
Matlin, Marlee, 56

N
National Institute for Occupational
Safety and Health, 29
noise, 27–30
non-organic hearing loss (NOHL), 21

O
otoacoustic emissions (OAE), 20

P
pregnancy, 24, 25, 31–32

pretended or faked deafness, 21
preventing deafness, 31–33
Pride, Curtis, 56
pure tone tests, 17, 19–20

R
Rh disease, 25

S
Self Help for Hard of Hearing Persons
(SHHH), 56
sensorineural deafness, 20–21, 23, 25, 41
and Rh disease, 25
signing, 34, 36, 37–40, 46
speech-reading, 34, 36–38
social interaction, 47–50
sound, 9, 11, 15
pitch, 10
vibrations, 9–11, 16, 18, 21, 27
sound waves, 10
surgery, 44

T
telephone device (TTD), 45–46
teletypewriter (TTY), 45–46
toxoplasmosis, 25, 31

W
Whitestone, Heather, 54

About the Author

Carol Basinger is a counselor, educator, and writer who has worked extensively with the deaf.

Photo Credits

Cover photo and p. 2 © FPG; pp.10, 37 © Archive Photos; pp. 12, 17, 26, 48 © Custom Medical; pp. 14, 28, 35, 44 by Kristen Artz; p.30 © Sports Chrome USA; pp. 52, 54 © The Everett Collection.

Layout and Design

Michael J. Caroleo